THE
UNIVERSE
IN YOU

AN INNER JOURNEY GUIDED BY
RUMI

TRANSLATIONS BY
OMID ARABIAN

For Mojdeh

{ In Gratitude }

This book came out of a course I have conducted for the past five years. I am therefore deeply grateful to all those who have attended and/or supported the course and shared their insights on these poems.

I am also grateful to the artist whose sublime drawings accompany these translations.

Above all, I am grateful to the spirit of Rumi, and to A.M.S. for opening my heart's eyes to this spirit.

~ O.A.

POEMS

The poems that follow are selections from *Divan-e Shams-e Tabrizi*, which comprises the collected poems of Jalaaleddin Mohammad Balkhi, known as Rumi (1207 - 1273 CE). The source poem for each translation appears in the original Farsi on the facing page.

While any act of translation inherently involves some degree of subjective interpretation, I have striven to keep as much as possible to the letter of Rumi's verses, not just to their spirit.

Readers are invited to delve into this collection with an open heart, and use Rumi's mystical poems as vehicles for their own inquiry into the great metaphysical questions of existence - the *who*, *what*, *when*, *where*, *& why* of the self and the universe.

{ 1 }

Where have you come from?
Do you know?
From within that glorious sanctum.

Search your memory -
do you recall at all
that sweet, spiritual state?

Then you've forgotten all that!
And so, you are bewildered
and wandering...

You sell your soul
for a fistful of soil!
Is that a fair trade?
Is this all you're worth?

Return the soil,
and know your own value!
You are no servant, no slave -
you are Lord, you are King.

Towards you,
from the heavens
they have come:
beautiful, joyous, hidden beings.

{ ۱ }

ز کجا آمدهای میدانی
ز میان حرم سبحانی

یاد کن هیچ به یادت آید
آن مقامات خوش روحانی

پس فراموش شدستت آنها
لاجرم خیره و سرگردانی

جان فروشی به یکی مشتی خاک
این چه بیع است بدین ارزانی

بازده خاک و بدان قیمت خود
نی غلامی ملکی سلطانی

جهت تو ز فلک آمدهاند
خوبرویان خوش پنهانی

{ 2 }

O tribe of Hajj* pilgrims, where are you?
Where are you?
The Beloved is right here!
Come, come.

Your Beloved lives where you live -
you are adjoined.
In the desert,
wandering,
what do you seek?

If you see the Beloved's faceless face,
you are the house
and the master of the house;
you are Ka'beh.

Ten times
you traveled that road to that house;
just once,
come through this house
and ascend to the roof!

That house is quite fine,
you've spoken of its attributes –
show some sign
of the Master of that house!

If you've seen that Garden,
where is your bouquet of flowers?
If you are from God's ocean,
where is the pearl of your essence?

Nontheless,
may your toil become your treasure –
alas, the veil upon your treasure
is you.

*Hajj is a pilgrimage undertaken by devout Muslims to perform a series of rituals in &
around Islam's holiest city, Mecca. This includes the act of walking seven times around
the Ka'beh, a small cube-shaped building regarded by many as 'the house of God'.

{ ۲ }

ای قوم به حج رفته کجایید کجایید
معشوق همین جاست بیایید بیایید

معشوق تو همسایه و دیوار به دیوار
در بادیه سرگشته شما در چه هوایید

گر صورت بی‌صورت معشوق ببینید
هم خواجه و هم خانه و هم کعبه شمایید

ده بار از آن راه بدان خانه برفتید
یک بار از این خانه بر این بام برآیید

آن خانه لطیفست نشان‌هاش بگفتید
از خواجه‌ی آن خانه نشانی بنمایید

یک دسته‌ی گل کو اگر آن باغ بدیدید
یک گوهر جان کو اگر از بحر خدایید

با این همه آن رنج شما گنج شما باد
افسوس که بر گنج شما پرده شمایید

{ 3 }

Each breath
that you are with yourself,
the Beloved is as a thorn to you;
and each breath
that you are without yourself,
oh, what the Beloved can do for you!

Each breath
that you are with yourself,
you are prey to mosquitoes;
and each breath
that you are without yourself,
elephants can be your prey.

Each breath
that you are with yourself,
you are bound
to a cloud of sadness;
and each breath
that you are without yourself,
the moon will be by your side.

Each breath
that you are with yourself,
the Beloved evades you;
and each breath
that you are without yourself,
the Beloved's wine will flow to you.

Each breath
that you are with yourself,
you are depressed, like autumn;
and each breath
that you are without yourself,
Winter will be like Spring to you.

All of your restlessness
is from your demand for rest -
seek without rest,
and peace will come to you.

آن نفسی که باخودی، یار چو خار آیدت
وآن نفسی که بی‌خودی، یار چه کار آیدت

آن نفسی که باخودی خود تو شکار پشه‌ای
وآن نفسی که بی‌خودی پیل شکار آیدت

آن نفسی که باخودی بسته‌ی ابر غصه‌ای
وآن نفسی که بی‌خودی مه به کنار آیدت

آن نفسی که باخودی یار کناره می‌کند
وآن نفسی که بی‌خودی باده‌ی یار آیدت

آن نفسی که باخودی همچو خزان فسرده‌ای
وآن نفسی که بی‌خودی دی چو بهار آیدت

جمله‌ی بی‌قراریت از طلب قرار توست
طالب بی‌قرار شو تا که قرار آیدت

جمله‌ی ناگوارشت از طلب گوارش است
ترک گوارش ار کنی زهر گوار آیدت

جمله‌ی بی‌مرادیت از طلب مراد توست
ور نه همه مرادها همچو نثار آیدت

عاشق جور یار شو عاشق مهر یار نی
تا که نگار نازگر عاشق زار آیدت

خسرو شرق شمس‌دین از تبریز چون رسد
از مه و از ستاره‌ها والله عار آیدت

{ 3 cont. }

All of your bitterness
is from the demand for sweetness -
if you abandon that demand,
even venom will taste sweet.

You remain unfulfilled
as long as you demand fulfillment -
otherwise, all fulfillment
will come effortlessly to you.

Fall in love
with the Beloved's torments,
not just her affections;
then the coy beauty
will come to you,
desperately in love.

Once the king of the East,
Shamseddin*,
arrives from Tabriz,
you will, by God, shun
even the moon and the stars!

*Shamseddin of Tabriz, 'Shams' for short, was Rumi's master and, for many years,
his inseparable companion. The word 'Shams', rooted in Arabic, means 'sun'.

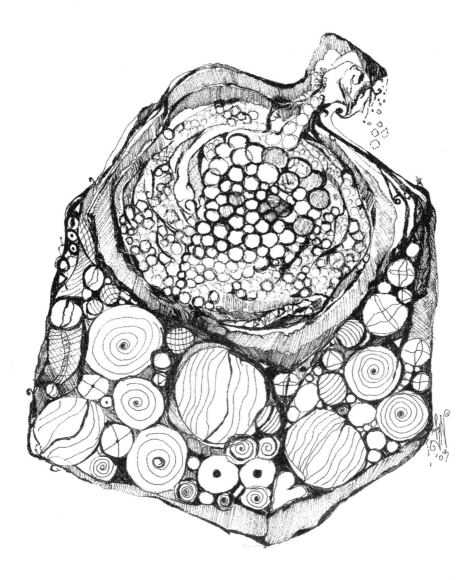

{ 4 }

Even if this world is full of thorns,
the Lover's heart is a meadow of blooming flowers.

And even if the great wheel ceases to turn,
the Lover's world is always at work.

Everyone may be steeped in sorrow,
while the Lover's soul remains
graceful, joyous, and swift.

Wherever there is a dead candle, bring it to the Lover -
a hundred thousand rays of light are his!

And if the Lover is alone, he is not truly alone -
he is mated with the hidden Beloved.

Lovers' wine ferments out from within their chest;
Love's partner resides in the world of mysteries.

The Lover is not satisfied with a hundred pledges -
for charmers are full of deceit.

And even if you see a Lover suffering, in need,
don't you know, that his Beloved is attending to his need?

Ride love's horse, and think nothing of the journey -
for love's horse knows the way quite well ...
in one charge, with one movement
it delivers you to the next station -
even if the road is not smooth.

But the Lover's spirit does not feed on grass!
Its sustenance is wine.

Through Shamseddin of Tabriz you will find
a heart that is drunken,
and quite aware.

اگر عالم همه پرخار باشد
دل عاشق همه گلزار باشد

وگر بی‌کار گردد چرخ گردون
جهان عاشقان بر کار باشد

همه غمگین شوند و جان عاشق
لطیف و خرم و عیار باشد

به عاشق ده تو هر جا شمع مرده‌ست
که او را صد هزار انوار باشد

وگر تنهاست عاشق نیست تنها
که با معشوق پنهان یار باشد

شراب عاشقان از سینه جوشد
حریف عشق در اسرار باشد

به صد وعده نباشد عشق خرسند
که مکر دلبران بسیار باشد

وگر بیمار بینی عاشقی را
نه شاهد بر سر بیمار باشد

سوار عشق شو وز ره میندیش
که اسب عشق بس رهوار باشد

به یک حمله تو را منزل رساند
اگر چه راه ناهموار باشد

علف خواری نداند جان عاشق
که جان عاشقان خمار باشد

ز شمس الدین تبریزی بیابی
دلی کو مست و بس هشیار باشد

{ 5 }

Stealthily you go,
like life, within my life;
you are my graceful cypress,
the splendor of my garden.

Go as you go,
but not without me!
O life of life,
don't go without body;
and never leave my sight -
for you are my shining flame.

I will tear through the seven skies,
and sail through the seven seas
when you look beguilingly
into my wandering soul.

When you appeared to me,
piety and heresy
both fell at my feet;
seeing you is my religion -
your face is my faith.

Because of you,
I've lost my bearings -
no food, no sleep;
you are my Joseph - come;
joyously, drunkenly come.

By your grace,
I became as life itself,
unseen even by myself.
It is your essence that resides,
unseen,
within my unseen self.

Because of you
the flower blooms,
tearing through its garment;
you intoxicate the narcissus*;
the branches are pregnant of
you -
you, my endless garden.

One moment,
you set me on fire;
another moment
you pull me into the garden;
you pull me toward the light -
so that my eyes open.

You, the life before all lives!
You, the mine before all mines!
You, the one before any other!
You are mine, you are mine.

No soil is our abode;
no fear, if the body crumbles;
no sky limits my soaring vision...
union with you
is my seventh heaven.

{ Note: This is a segment of a longer poem. }

*Narcissus: A flower whose more common name is daffodil.

دزدیده چون جان می روی اندر میان جان من
سرو خرامان منی ای رونق بستان من

چون میروی بی من مرو ای جان جان بی تن مرو
وز چشم من بیرون مشو ای شعله ی تابان من

هفت آسمان را بردرم وز هفت دریا بگذرم
چون دلبرانه بنگری در جان سرگردان من

تا آمدی اندر برم شد کفر و ایمان چاکرم
ای دیدن تو دین من وی روی تو ایمان من

بی پا و سر کردی مرا بی خواب و خور کردی مرا
سرمست و خندان اندرآ ای یوسف کنعان من

از لطف تو چون جان شدم وز خویشتن پنهان شدم
ای هست تو پنهان شده در هستی پنهان من

گل جامه در از دست تو ای چشم نرگس مست تو
ای شاخه ها آبست تو ای باغ بی پایان من

یك لحظه داغم می کشی یك دم به باغم می کشی
پیش چراغم می کشی تا وا شود چشمان من

ای جان پیش از جانها وی کان پیش از کانها
ای آن پیش از آنها ای آن من ای آن من

منزلگه ما خاك نی گر تن بریزد باك نی
اندیشه ام افلاك نی ای وصل تو کیوان من

{ 6 }

I've come
to pull you by the ear
towards myself -
to steal your heart,
take you out of yourself
and seat you in my heart,
in my soul.

I've come
like the joyous spring
towards you,
o flowering tree -
to give your flowers bloom,
then take you in my arms.

I've come
to give you splendor
in this abode,
and take you
beyond the heavens
like lovers' prayers.

You've stolen a kiss;
I've come to reclaim it -
so give it gladly,
or I will take it back.

Flowers?
You are the flower!
You speak the Word!
If others don't recognize you,
I do -
for you are me.

You are my heart and my soul;
you sing my song of expansion;
become expansion,
nothing else -
and I will sing you to my heart.

{ continued }

آمده‌ام که تا به خود گوش کشان کشانمت
بی دل و بی خودت کنم در دل و جان نشانمت

آمده‌ام بهار خوش پیش تو ای درخت گل
تا که کنار گیرمت خوش خوش می‌فشانمت

آمده‌ام که تا تو را جلوه دهم در این سرا
همچو دعای عاشقان فوق فلک رسانمت

آمده‌ام که بوسه‌ای از صنمی ربوده‌ای
بازبده به خوشدلی خواجه که واستانمت

گل چه بود که گل تویی ناطق امر قل تویی
گر دگری نداندت چون تو منی بدانمت

جان و روان من تویی فاتحه خوان من تویی
فاتحه شو تو یک سری تا که به دل بخوانمت

صید منی شکار من گر چه ز دام جسته‌ای
جانب دام بازرو ور نروی برانمت

نی که تو شیرزاده‌ای در تن آهویی نهان
من ز حجاب آهوی یک ره رهه بگذرانمت

زخم پذیر و پیش رو چون سپر شجاعتی
گوش به غیر زه مده تا چو کمان خمانمت

از حد خاک تا بشر چند هزار منزلست
شهر به شهر بردمت بر سر ره نمانمت

هیچ مگو و کف مکن سر مگشای دیگ را
نیک بجوش و صبر کن زانک همی‌پزانمت

گوی منی و می‌دوی در چوگان حکم من
در پی تو همی‌دوم گر چه که می‌دوانمت

21

{ 6 cont. }

You are my quest,
you are my quarry -
though you've flown the coop;
head back towards it,
or I'll chase you there.

By birth, you are a lion -
a lion hidden
in the body of a deer;
I will pass you
right through that veil.

Allow the blows
and move forward -
you are bravery's shield!
Yield to the power
that shoots the arrow -
so that I can bend you
like a bow.

From the rank of Soil
to the Human form,
thousands of stations stand;
I took you
from one to the next -
I won't leave you stranded.

Say nothing,
and don't froth -
don't blow the lid;
simmer, patiently
and I will ripen you,
bit by bit.

You are the polo ball
and I am the mallet;
the game is mine,
and yet,
I am the one
running after you.

{ 7 }

I was dead -
I came alive.
I was tears -
I became laughter.
Love's wealth arrived,
and I became
everlasting fortune.

My eyes no longer crave -
they've seen enough.
mine is a brave soul;
mine is the lion's courage;
now I am the shining Venus.

She said,
"You are not insane -
you are not worthy
of this house."
I went and became insane -
insane enough to be in chains.

She said,
"You are not drunken!
Go!
You are not of this league!"
I went, and became drunken,
brimming with joy.

She said,
"You are not yet killed -
not dissolved in ecstasy!"
I collapsed and died
before her life-giving face.

She said,
"You are too clever -
muddled in fancies and doubt!"
I went and lost my mind,
lost all my bearings...
and detached from all.

She said,
"You've become a candle -
the one to whom
these masses pray."
I am not the masses.
I am not their candle.
I became a candle's smoke,
and scattered.

She said,
"You are a scholar,
you are a preacher,
a commander, and a leader!"
I am no more -
not a scholar, not a leader -
I am at your command,
tending to your affairs.

She said,
"You are arrogant -
I will not give you my wings!"
In longing for her wings,
I shed my lofty feathers.

Then the new fortune said,
"Travel no more,
toil no more.
In grace and generosity,
I am headed for you."

{ Note: This is a segment of a longer poem. }

مرده بدم زنده شدم گریه بدم خنده شدم
دولت عشق آمد و من دولت پاینده شدم

دیدهِ ی سیر است مرا جان دلیر است مرا
زهره ی شیر است مرا زهره ی تابنده شدم

گفت که دیوانه نه‌ای لایق این خانه نه‌ای
رفتم و دیوانه شدم سلسله بندنده شدم

گفت که سرمست نه‌ای رو که از این دست نه‌ای
رفتم و سرمست شدم وز طرب آکنده شدم

گفت که تو کشته نه‌ای در طرب آغشته نه‌ای
پیش رخ زنده کنش کشته و افکنده شدم

گفت که تو زیرککی مست خیالی و شکی
گول شدم هول شدم وز همه برکنده شدم

گفت که تو شمع شدی قبله ی این جمع شدی
جمع نیم شمع نیم دود پراکنده شدم

گفت که شیخی و سری پیش رو و راهبری
شیخ نیم پیش نیم امر تو را بنده شدم

گفت که با بال و پری من پر و بالت ندهم
در هوس بال و پرش بی‌پر و پرکنده شدم

گفت مرا دولت نو راه مرو رنجه مشو
زانک من از لطف و کرم سوی تو آینده شدم

{ 8 }

O lover, abandon deceit!
Become insane, become insane.
Become a moth, and like the moth,
enter into the burning flame.

Estrange everything familiar,
and leave your earthly house in ruins;
then, come in to the house of love;
with lovers live, become their mate.

In Seven waters cleanse your chest
of hate and grudges, like a fawn;
and then, unto the wine of love,
become a cup, become a cup.

You must become nothing but life
to be worthy of life's essence;
toward the drunkards if you go,
become intoxicated too.

The earring on each beauty's ear
has turned into her confidant -
to hear the Beloved's voice,
become a gem, become a gem.

And when your soul begins to soar
from hearing my sweet mythic tale,
like lovers, vanish from this world -
become a myth, become a song.

You are the darkness of the grave -
become the night when light descends;
and like that celebrated night,
become the realm where spirits dwell.

Your thoughts take flight this way and that,
and take you with them, here and there;
surpass your thoughts, transcend your mind
and lead the way, like divine will.

Our base desires and passing whims
have placed a lock upon our hearts;
become a key; or better yet,
become the key's unlocking teeth.

{ continued }

حیلت رها کن عاشقا دیوانه شو دیوانه شو
واندر دل آتش درآ پروانه شو پروانه شو

هم خویش را بیگانه کن هم خانه را ویرانه کن
وانگه بیا با عاشقان هم خانه شو هم خانه شو

رو سینه را چون سینها هفت آب شو از کینها
وانگه شراب عشق را پیمانه شو پیمانه شو

باید که جمله جان شوی تا لایق جانان شوی
گر سوی مستان میروی مستانه شو مستانه شو

آن گوشوار شاهدان هم صحبت عارض شده
آن گوش و عارض بایدت دردانه شو دردانه شو

چون جان تو شد در هوا ز افسانه ی شیرین ما
فانی شو و چون عاشقان افسانه شو افسانه شو

تو لیلۀ القبری برو تا لیلۀ القدری شوی
چون قدر مر ارواح را کاشانه شو کاشانه شو

اندیشه ات جایی رود وانگه تو را آنجا کشد
ز اندیشه بگذر چون قضا پیشانه شو پیشانه شو

قفلی بُود میل و هوا
بنهاده بر دلهای ما
مفتاح شو مفتاح را
دندانه شو
دندانه شو

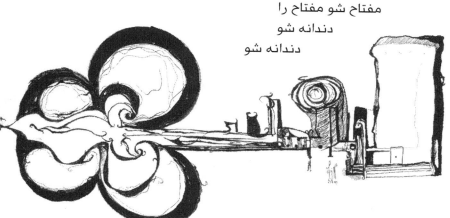

{ 8 cont. }

King Solomon is asking you
to hear the message of the birds:
when you're a trap, they run from you -
become a nest, become a nest.

If the Beloved shows her face,
fill yourself of her, mirrorlike;
and if she lets down her sweet curls,
become a comb, become a comb.

You travel to and fro, like rooks;
all by yourself, just like a pawn;
how long, like bishops, on the skew?
Become all-knowing, like a king.

So gratefully, you gave love gifts;
rare souvenirs, expensive things...
forget those things, and give yourself!
Become the gift, the grateful gift.

Awhile, you were the elements,
and then the plants and animals;
since you are now a human life,
become more like the life of life!

You are a songbird - but how long
will you keep flying here and there?
Fly to the coop, abandon words,
let go of speech, and become hushed.

گوید سلیمان مر ترا بشنو لسان الطیر را
دامی و مرغ از تو رمد رو لانه شو لانه شو

گر چهره بنماید صنم پر شو از او چون آینه
ور زلف بگشاید صنم رو شانه شو رو شانه شو

تا کی دو شاخه چون رخی تا کی چو بیذق کم تکی
تاکی چو فرزین کژ روی فرزانه شو فرزانه شو

شکرانه دادی عشق را از تحفه ها و مالها
هل مال را خود را بده شکرانه شو شکرانه شو

یك مدتی ارکان بدی یك مدتی حیوان بدی
یك مدتی چون جان شدی جانانه شو جانانه شو

ای ناطقه بربام و در تاکی روی در خانه پر
نطق زبان را ترک کن بی چانه شو بی چانه شو

{ 9 }

O my dear heart, sit with the one
who draws knowledge straight from the heart;
and only go beneath that tree
that always has fresh-blooming buds.

Do not meander aimlessly
among these perfume-merchants' stalls;
but dwell instead within the shop
of one who has sugar in stock.

Unless you have your own true scale,
you'll be quick prey to any thief -
he'll fashion lovely forgeries,
and you'll believe that they are gold.

The thief will seat you by the door,
and say that he will soon return;
but don't keep waiting at the door -
remember: the house has two doors.

Don't bring your bowl and meekly sit
by each and every boiling pot;
for each and every boiling pot
conceals yet something else inside.

Not every cane is sugar-filled;
not every low precedes a high;
not every eye can truly see;
not every ocean has its pearls.

O nightingale, do sing your song;
and rest assured that drunken songs
among hard stones and granite rocks
do leave a mark, do leave a mark.

If you don't fit, then give your head -
for if the thread declines to pass
within the needle's narrow eye,
it is because it has a head.

{ continued }

دلا نزد کسی بنشین که او از دل خبر دارد
به زیر آن درختی رو که او گل‌های تر دارد

در این بازار عطاران مرو هر سو چو بی‌کاران
به دکان کسی بنشین که در دکان شکر دارد

ترازو گر نداری پس تو را زو ره زند هر کس
یکی قلبی بیاراید تو پنداری که زر دارد

تو را بر در نشاند او به طراری که می‌آید
تو منشین منتظر بر در که آن خانه دو در دارد

به هر دیگی که می‌جوشد میاور کاسه و منشین
که هر دیگی که می‌جوشد درون چیزی دگر دارد

نه هر کلکی شکر دارد نه هر زیری زبر دارد
نه هر چشمی نظر دارد نه هر بحری گهر دارد

بنال ای بلبل دستان ازیرا ناله‌ی مستان
میان صخره و خارا اثر دارد اثر دارد

بنه سر گر نمی‌گنجی که اندر چشمه‌ی سوزن
اگر رشته نمی‌گنجد از آن باشد که سر دارد

چراغست این دل بیدار به زیر دامنش می‌دار
از این باد و هوا بگذر هوایش شور و شر دارد

چو تو از باد بگذشتی مقیم چشمه‌ای گشتی
حریف همدمی گشتی که آبی بر جگر دارد

چو آبت بر جگر باشد درخت سبز را مانی
که میوه نو دهد دایم درون دل سفر دارد

{ 9 cont. }

This wakened heart's your guiding light -
conceal it well beneath your robe,
and travel through these winds and airs
so full of turmoil and decay.

When you've passed through those gusty winds,
you'll dwell beside the water's source,
and find a mate who shares your breath
and drinks from that life-giving spring.

And when that water circulates,
you're like a tree that's ever-green
and always bears the freshest fruits -
it journeys deep into the heart.

{ 10 }

In wonderment, I cried out:
Where does my drunken heart go?
Silence,
said the King of kings,
it goes toward me.

I said:
But you are with me!
You speak to me from within –
so why does my heart travel
boldly in the world without?

The King said:
Your heart is mine;
it's my Rostam*,
my champion -
and so it goes
to fight delusions.

Any direction it goes,
fortune follows it as well -
say nothing,
and let it travel
wherever it intends.

Sometimes,
like rays of the sun,
it brings treasures to the earth;
sometimes,
like prophets' prayers,
it spirals up, heavenward.

Follow the heart's expressions
so, within you, you can see
meadows grow
and flowers bloom,
a river of kindness and faith.

What gives shape to all the world
is simple, and without shape;
what gives everything its worth
travels without feet,
and without a head.

The heart is like a window -
it's what gives the house its light;
the body goes toward decay -
the heart goes on, everlasting.

The heart raises rebellions,
the heart sheds emperors' blood;
the heart commingles with all -
though it travels singly.

Those who find
the divine magic in their heart,
will tear through Gemini's trap
and fly up to distant stars.

With this heart within yourself,
it's folly to hold the purse -
the purse is gone, disappeared -
and the soul follows the thief.

Between beloved and heart
there is always give and take -
though what goes before your eyes
is only the outer shell.

It's the sound
of the water-horse**
calling for you to come out -
come out of your house,
and see
how the water-horse goes forth.

---

* Rostam is the foremost hero of Ferdowsi's epic poem *Shahnameh* (10th C. CE).
**In Rumi's time, drinking water would be carried on horses through a town, and distributed among its residents. The horses often wore a bell to announce their arrival.

بانگ زدم من که دل مست کجا میرود
گفت شهنشه خموش جانب ما میرود

گفتم تو با منی دم ز درون میزنی
پس دل من از برون خیره چرا میرود

گفت که دل آن ماست رستم دستان ماست
سوی خیال خطا بهر غزا میرود

هر طرفی کو رود بخت از آن سو رود
هیچ مگو هر طرف خواهد تا میرود

گه مثل آفتاب گنج زمین میشود
گه چو دعای رسول سوی سما میرود

بر اثر دل برو تا تو ببینی درون
سبزه و گل میدمد جوی وفا میرود

صورت بخش جهان ساده و بی صورتست
آن سر و پای همه بی سر و پا میرود

دل مثل روزنست خانه بدو روشنست
تن به فنا میرود دل به بقا میرود

فتنه برانگیخت دل خون شهان ریخت دل
با همه آمیخت دل گر چه جدا میرود

سحر خدا آفرید در دل هر کس بدید
کیسه ی جوزا برید همچو سها میرود

با تو دلا ابلهیست کیسه نگه داشتن
کیسه شد وجان پی کیسه ربا میرود

دایم دلدار را با دل و جان ماجراست
پوست برونیست اینک پیش شما میرود

اسب سقایست این بانگ درآیست این
بانگ کنان کز برون اسب سقا میرود

{ 11 }

I tried them all,
but none brought me more joy
than you;
I dove into the ocean, deep -
and could not find a pearl
like you.

I tasted wine
from a thousand casks -
but none like your rebellious wine
touched my lips,
or went to my head.

No wonder that in my heart
bouquets of jasmine are in bloom;
for no flower with all your grace
had ever before appeared to me.

Following you,
I left behind my own desires
for a few days;
and after that,
no desire remained
beyond my reach.

For two or three days
I became a servant
of your sovereignty;
and after that,
there was no king
who did not become my servant.

My wisdom told me:
Fly away
from the passengers of this world -
why do you wait,
with broken legs
for your passenger to arrive?

When the dove within my heart flew
from my body
toward your roof,
I cried out, like a nightingale:
Where is my dove?
Will it return?

Then I flew out,
like a hawk
after my dove, into the air;
and then I saw, before my eyes,
the mythic Simorgh and Homaay.*

Farewell to you,
distressed body;
to you, and to my regretful heart -
for until I was free of both,
that other heart
would not arrive.

*Simorgh: mythical bird who is said to be the source of all wisdom.
Homaay: mythical bird who flies over the heads of those who will be King.

همه را بیازمودم ز تو خوشترم نیامد
چو فروشدم به دریا چو تو گوهرم نیامد

سر خنبه‌ها گشادم ز هزار خم چشیدم
چو شراب سرکش تو به لب و سرم نیامد

چه عجب که در دل من گل یاسمن بخندد
که سمن بری لطیفی چو تو در برم نیامد

ز پیت مراد خود را دو سه روز ترک کردم
چه مراد ماند زان پس که میسرم نیامد

دو سه روز شاهیت را چو شدم غلام و چاکر
به جهان نماند شاهی که چو چاکرم نیامد

خردم گفت برپر ز مسافران گردون
چه شکسته پا نشستی که مسافرم نیامد

چو پرید سوی بامت ز تنم کبوتر دل
به فغان شدم چو بلبل که کبوترم نیامد

چو پی کبوتر دل به هوا شدم چو بازان
چه همای ماند و عنقا که برابرم نیامد

برو ای تن پریشان تو وان دل پشیمان
که ز هر دو تا نرستم دل دیگرم نیامد

{ 12 }

Strive, o lovers, strive
so when there's no life left in the flesh,
your heart will fly skyward -
and not, like the body, remain mired in weight.

In the water of knowingness
cleanse your heart and soul from grime -
so that longing for the world of soil
does not remain.

Isn't love the essence
of all that is in the world?
Besides love, eternal,
whatever you see does not remain.

Your end is like the dawn,
and your lifetime like dusk -
fly toward a different sky,
one that does not resemble this sky.

The way to that sky is within,
so flutter the wings of love -
with those wings strong,
the yearning for a ladder does not remain.

Don't look at the world from without
as the world is within your eyes -
once you close your two eyes,
this fleeting world does not remain.

Your heart is like a roof
and your senses, the gutter;
drink from the roof -
as gutters do not remain.

Take in this poem fully
from the slate of your heart;
don't look at my words -
for lips and words do not remain.

The human body is a bow;
the breath and the word are arrows;
when the arrows and quiver are gone
the bow's action does not remain.

هله عاشقان بکوشید که چو جسم و جان نماند
دلتان به چرخ پرد چو بدن گران نماند

دل و جان به آب حکمت ز غبارها بشویید
هله تا دو چشم حسرت سوی خاکدان نماند

نه که هر چه در جهانست نه که عشق جان آنست
جز عشق هر چه بینی همه جاودان نماند

عدم تو همچو مشرق اجل تو همچو مغرب
سوی آسمان دیگر که به آسمان نماند

ره آسمان درونست پر عشق را بجنبان
پر عشق چون قوی شد غم نردبان نماند

تو مبین جهان ز بیرون که جهان درون دیده‌ست
چو دو دیده را ببستی ز جهان جهان نماند

دل تو مثال بامست و حواس ناودان‌ها
تو ز بام آب می‌خور که چو ناودان نماند

تو ز لوح دل فروخوان به تمامی این غزل را
منگر تو در زبانم که لب و زبان نماند

تن آدمی کمان و نفس و سخن چو تیرش
چو برفت تیر و ترکش عمل کمان نماند

{ 13 }

Don't turn to look
at every beggar that beckons -
you belong to me!
Don't sell yourself
at such a low price -
you are priceless!

Part the waters with your staff -
you are today's Moses!
Tear through the cloak of fog -
You are of the light,
the same light as Mohammad!

Shatter the mirrors of the 'virtuous'-
you are the dazzling Joseph!
Blow the breath of life
like Christ -
you, too, are of that air!

Break away
from the unscrupulous;
don't fall
for the deceit of ghouls!
You are of noble origin;
you are from the highest high!

By spirit, you are deathless -
imperishable;
magnificent from within!
You belong to the glorious;
you are of divine radiance!

What have you seen
of your own beauty?
You are still veiled...
One dawn, like the sun,
you will arise
from within yourself.

{ continued }

{ ۱۳ }

منگر به هر گدایی که تو خاص از آن مایی
مفروش خویش ارزان که تو بس گران بهایی

به عصا شکاف دریا که تو موسی زمانی
بدران قبای مه را که ز نور مصطفایی

بشکن سبوی خوبان که تو یوسف جمالی
چو مسیح دم روان کن که تو نیز از آن هوایی

بسکل ز بی‌اصولان مشنو فریب غولان
که تو از شریف اصلی که تو از بلند جایی

تو به روح بی‌زوالی ز درونه باجمالی
تو از آن ذوالجلالی تو ز پرتو خدایی

تو هنوز ناپدیدی ز جمال خود چه دیدی
سحری چو آفتابی ز درون خود برآیی

تو چنین نهان دریغی که مهی به زیر میغی
بدران تو میغ تن را که مهی و خوش لقایی

چو تو لعل کان ندارد چو تو جان جهان ندارد
که جهان کاهش است این و تو جان جان فزایی

تو چو باز پای بسته تن تو چو کنده بر پا
تو به چنگ خویش باید که گره ز پا گشایی

چه خوش است زر خالص چو به آتش اندرآید
چو کند درون آتش هنر و گهرنمایی

مگریز ای برادر تو ز شعله‌های آذر
ز برای امتحان را چه شود اگر درآیی

به خدا تو را نسوزد رخ تو چو زر فروزد
که خلیل زاده‌ای تو ز قدیم آشنایی

{ 13 cont. }

It's a shame that you are shrouded this way -
like the moon under a cloud;
tear through the cloud of body!
You are the moon, so beautiful!

No mine has a jewel like you!
This world has no life like you!
For this is the world of decay -
and you are life-giving life.

You are like a hawk
whose feet are tethered,
weighed down by the body;
it's with your own claws
that you must untie the knots.

How joyous is pure gold
when it enters the fire!
For it is within the flames
that gold shows its essence and its skills.

So don't flee from the flames -
what could happen
if you step into the fire
and test it out?

It will not burn you, I swear!
Your face will glow like gold -
for you are born of Abraham,*
ancient wisdom is yours.

Rise up, out of the soil -
you are a lofty tree;
fly up to the mountain's peak -
you are a royal bird.

You are sugar, so spread sweetness!
Yours is a grand music of joy -
so play the reed
and spread the wealth.

*Reference is made to a story in the Qor'an, wherein Abraham is set on fire for being
an iconoclast, but does not burn.

تو ز خاک سر برآور که درخت سربلندی
تو بپر به قاف قربت که شریفتر همایی

شکری شکرفشان کن که تو قند نوشقندی
بنواز نای دولت که عظیم خوش نوایی

{ 14 }

Beginning-less light
of which you've been bred
is instilled, abundantly,
within you.

Gaze joyously
upon all things
like the sun,
so they can thaw -
for they are compressed.

Look toward the trees
o newness of Spring -
for they have all wilted
in mad winter's cold.

Part your lips
and call forth
the greatness of Christ -
for false prophets' treachery
has deadened them all.

Break this half-sober state
that everyone is in -
for they've already had
a taste of your wine.

Give eternal life
as an antidote -
for mortality's poison
has tainted them all.

Tear through the curtain of night,
like dawn -
for they are all shrouded
by hundreds of veils.

Enough - be silent,
hold your hundred tongues -
for they have not even brought
a single ear.

{ ۱٤ }

زان ازلی نور که پروردهاند
در تو زیادت نظری کردهاند

خوش بنگر در همه خورشیدوار
تا بگدازند که افسردهاند

سوی درختان نگر ای نوبهار
کز دی دیوانه بپژمردهاند

لب بگشا هیکل عیسی بخوان
کز دم دجال جفا مردهاند

بشکن امروز خمار همه
کز می تو چاشنیی بردهاند

درده تریاق حیات ابد
کاین همگان زهر فنا خوردهاند

همچو سحر پردهٔ شب را بدر
کاین همه محجوب دو صد پردهاند

بس کن و خاموش مشو صدزبان
چونک یکی گوش نیاوردهاند

{ 15 }

Whatever happens in this world,
where is your work?
Where is your task?
If idol-worship rules both worlds,
where's your beauty,
to trump them all?

If famine overtakes the world -
no bread to eat,
no bowls to fill -
o, king of both seen and unseen.
where's your storehouse,
your measuring cup?

And even if the world's all thorns,
teeming with scorpions and snakes,
o, happiness, o joy of life:
where is your garden,
in full bloom?

If generosity is dead
and selfishness has killed them all,
o, my dear heart,
my precious eyes:
where is your treasure
and your gems?

And even if the dark of hell
has swallowed both
the sun and moon,
o strength of ears,
o spark of eyes,
where is your flame?
Where is your light?

Even if there are no jewelers,
and no one out to buy their wares,
why don't you make
your own true wealth?
Where is your cloud
that rains down pearls?

And even if there are no mouths,
and even if there are no tongues,
no breath to speak of mysteries,
when will your hidden wisdom flow?

But never mind,
for I am drunk
and yearning for that lovely face;
it's getting late, so quickly come -
where can we find
your house of wine?

Look at me closely,
drunk with joy,
our hearts are one,
our hands entwined -
if you are not a drinker too,
then where's your mantle?
Where's your cloak?

An outsider is poised to steal
away from the eternal drunks -
so why are you not standing guard?
Where is your blade,
your gallows' rope?

Silence, O spreader of words!
Only the silent truly hear.
Don't join the ranks
of babbling mobs -
Where is your Word?
Where is your Truth?

کار جهان هر چه شود کار تو کو بار تو کو
گر دو جهان بتکده شد آن بت عیار تو کو

گیر که قحط است جهان نیست دگر کاسه و نان
ای شه پیدا و نهان کیله و انبار تو کو

گیر که خار است جهان کژدم و مار است جهان
ای طرب و شادی جان گلشن و گلزار تو کو

گیر که خود مرد سخا کشت بخیلی همه را
ای دل و ای دیده‌ی ما خلعت و ادرار تو کو

گیر که خورشید و قمر هر دو فروشد به سقر
ای مدد سمع و بصر شعله و انوار تو کو

گیر که خود جوهری نیست پی مشتری
چون نکنی سروری ابر گهربار تو کو

گیر دهانی نبود گفت زبانی نبود
تا دم اسرار زند جوشش اسرار تو کو

هین همه بگذار که ما مست وصالیم و لقا
بی‌گه شد زود بیا خانه‌ی خمار تو کو

تیز نگر مست مرا همدل و همدست مرا
گر نه خرابی و خرف جبه و دستار تو کو

بر سر مستان ابد خارجیی راه زند
شحنگیی چون نکنی زخم تو کو دار تو کو

خامش ای حرف فشان درخور گوش خمشان
ترجمه‌ی خلق مکن حالت و گفتار تو کو

{ 16 }

I've come again,
like a new Spring,
to shatter every prison's lock;
to break
the very claws and teeth
of this man-eating spinning world.

I will pour water on the fires
of the seven arid stars
that swallow up the earthly ones -
I'll break their pride,
like so much air

Like a falcon,
I've flown again
from that beginning-less King
out toward this realm of ruin
to break the parrot-eating owl.

Right from the start,
I've made a vow:
to pour my life unto the King -
and if I ever break that vow,
my back should break,
my life should end!

If the gardens of the heedless
are green a day or two,
don't fret -
for I will, in my hidden ways,
break their principles at the root.

Today I am the viceroy
holding the order and the sword -
to break the necks
of those who stand
against the glory of the King.

{ continued }

بازآمدم چون عید نو تا قفل زندان بشکنم
وین چرخ مردم خوار را چنگال و دندان بشکنم

هفت اختر بی‌آب را کاین خاکیان را می خورند
هم آب بر آتش زنم هم بادهاشان بشکنم

از شاه بی‌آغاز من پران شدم چون باز من
تا جغد طوطی خوار را در دیر ویران بشکنم

ز آغاز عهدی کرده‌ام کاین جان فدای شه کنم
بشکسته بادا پشت جان گر عهد و پیمان بشکنم

روزی دو باغ طاغیان گر سبز بینی غم مخور
چون اصل‌های بیخشان از راه پنهان بشکنم

امروز همچون آصفم شمشیر و فرمان در کفم
تا گردن گردن کشان در پیش سلطان بشکنم

من نشکنم جز جور را یا ظالم بدغور را
گر ذره‌ای دارد نمك گبرم اگر آن بشکنم

هر جا یکی گویی بود چوگان وحدت وی برد
گویی که میدان نسپرد در زخم چوگان بشکنم

گشتم مقیم بزم او چون لطف دیدم عزم او
گشتم حقیر راه او تا ساق شیطان بشکنم

چون در کف سلطان شدم یك حبه بودم کان شدم
گردر ترازویم نهی می دان که میزان بشکنم

{ 16 cont. }

I break only brutality
and the torturing oppressor;
I'd be a traitor if I broke
what carries the flavor of life.

Wherever there's a polo ball
the mallet guides it to union;
and if a ball tries not to yield
I'll break it with a mallet's strike.

I saw grace as the King's intent,
so I entered into his feast;
I came humbly onto his path
so I could break the devil's legs.

And when he took me in his hands
I was a grain,
I'm now a mine;
and if you put me in a scale,
know
that I'll break that measure too.

{ Note: This is a segment of a longer poem. }

{ 17 }

Every moment,
with each breath,
a new messenger arrives
from the city of the Beloved -
with the joy of union,
with the king's wine-filled cup.

Consciousness itself applauds;
every particle
and all of existence
in a dance...
trees and flowers
bowing down
before the meadow.

It is of this breath
that the ocean is in upheaval,
the mountain is filled with gems.
the energy of life sings out,
and the spirit is humbled,
yearning.

Look, my far-sighted wisdom,
and see
the cup-bearer,
the wine-giver,
dark-haired and fair-skinned
bringing the divine wine;
heart and soul excited,
impatient.

Hear the good tidings
coming from every direction,
left and right:
good fortune is yours;
light and clarity are in place -
as long as you are sovereign.

Tear through the spinning veil
and partake in the divine feast;
drink from the water of life -
renew ...
and embrace that ethereal beauty.

For those who know
the state of joy,
what starts out as just a dream
will in the end become real -
once the Beloved appears.

آید هر دم رسول از طرف شهر یار
با فرح وصل دوست با قدح شهریار

دست زنان عقل کل رقص کنان جزو و کل
سجده کنان سرو و گل بر طرف سبزه زار

بحر از این دم به جوش کوه از این لعل پوش
نوح از این در خروش روح از این شرمسار

ای خرد دوربین ساقی چون حور بین
باده‌ی منصور بین جان و دلی بی‌قرار

بشنو از چپ و راست مژده سعادت تو راست
بخت صفا در صفاست تا تو توی اختیار

پرده‌ی گردون بدر نعمت جنت بخور
آب بزن بر جگر حور بکش در کنار

هر چه بر اصحاب حال باشد اول خیال
گردد آخر وصال چونك درآید نگار

{ 18 }

Last night,
my Beloved placed
a golden crown upon my head -
and from my head it shall not fall,
in spite of all your slaps and blows.

The eternal king and hatmaker
has placed the nightcap of his love
from his own head
upon my head -
and eternally, it remains.

And if my head and hat perish,
I will arise
like the full moon;
freed from its restraining shell,
my pearl will glitter brighter still.

Now here's my head,
and here's a mace -
so land a blow,
and test it out;
and if the bones break,
you will see:
I've more substance than the mind,
and more than just physical life.

Only a mindless nut will choose
the shell
instead of what's within -
for he has never had a taste
of my Beloved's sweet nectar.

Her sweet confection,
sugar-filled,
full of substance and nourishment,
sweetens my lips, my mouth, my throat,
and brings light into my eyes.

{ continued }

دی بر سرم تاج زری بنهاده است آن دلبرم
چندانک سیلی می زنی آن می نیفتد از سرم

شاه کله دوز ابد بر فرق من از فرق خود
شب پوش عشق خود نهد پاینده باشد لاجرم

ور سر نماند با کله من سر شوم جمله چو مه
زیرا که بی حقه و صدف رخشانتر آید گوهرم

اینک سر و گرز گران می زن برای امتحان
ور بشکند این استخوان از عقل و جان مغزینترم

آن جوز بی مغزی بود کو پوست بگزیده بود
او ذوق کی دیده بود از لوزی پیغامبرم

لوزینه ی پرجوز او پرشکر و پرلوز او
شیرین کند حلق و لبم نوری نهد در منظرم

چون مغز یابی ای پسر از پوست برداری نظر
در کوی عیسی آمدی دیگر نگویی کو خرم

ای جان من تا کی گله یک خر تو کم گیر از گله
در زفتی فارس نگر نی بارگیر لاغرم

زفتی عاشق را بدان از زفتی معشوق او
زیرا که کبر عاشقان خیزد ز الله اکبرم

ای دردهای آه گو اه گو اه مگو الله گو
از چه مگو از جان بگو ای یوسف جان پرورم

{ 18 cont. }

And when you discover the core,
you will discard both shell and bone -
you will enter the realm of Christ,
and no longer seek the ass*.

My dear,
how long will you complain?
The herd can do with one less ass!
So gaze upon the rider's heft
and not the scrawny carrier.

A lover's measure you can find
in his beloved's measureless size -
the lover's grandness arises
from the grandeur of the divine

O earthly pains,
don't moan and fret -
but speak the name of the divine!
You are Joseph, who nurtures life -
so speak of life,
not of the well.

*Reference is made to the accounts of Jesus' triumphal entry into Jerusalem, riding
upon a donkey.

{ 19 }

Praise love, praise love,
this love that is ours -
how pure, how good,
how beautiful it is.

How warm we are,
from this love, like the sun!
So hidden, so mystical,
yet so evident, it is.

We've fallen into it,
and in it we'll remain;
little do we know
what great upheaval it brings.

Praise the glorious moon,
and the wine that's with us -
it gives shape to the world,
and brings beauty to life.

The king of kings
rode down on his horse -
and hail the dust
that rose up as he arrived.

What passion,
what excitement
courses through the world
and animates everything!
So much has been done;
there's so much to be done!

From every street,
from every alley
a different smoke wafts up!
Once again,
a new enterprise,
a new creation is at hand!

There are no traps,
no chains to be seen -
so how are we bound,
how are we linked?
Oh, what chains and what ropes
are at work...

What image is it
reflected in our hearts?
So strange, so mysterious,
it comes from above.

Silent, silent,
so you are not discovered -
for strangers have taken over
every corner,
left and right.

زهی عشق زهی عشق که ما راست خدایا
چه نغزست و چه خوبست چه زیباست خدایا

چه گرمیم چه گرمیم از این عشق چو خورشید
چه پنهان و چه پنهان و چه پیداست خدایا

فتادیم فتادیم بدان سان که نخیزیم
ندانیم ندانیم چه غوغاست خدایا

زهی ماه زهی ماه زهی باده ی همراه
که جان را و جهان را بیاراست خدایا

فروریخت فروریخت شهنشاه سواران
زهی گرد زهی گرد که برخاست خدایا

زهی شور زهی شور که انگیخته عالم
زهی کار زهی بار که آن جاست خدایا

ز هر کوی ز هر کوی یکی دود دگرگون
دگربار دگربار چه سوداست خدایا

نه دامیست نه زنجیر همه بسته چراییم
چه بندست چه زنجیر که برپاست خدایا

چه نقشیست چه نقشیست در این تابه ی دلها
غریبست غریبست ز بالاست خدایا

خموشید خموشید که تا فاش نگردید
که اغیار گرفتست چپ و راست خدایا

{ 20 }

I'll gift my life
to lovers -
theirs is a joyful craving.
Worship love, young man,
everything else
is as the wind.

I am drunk,
with love's wine;
I am love's fire,
spreading, expanding;
step into these flames -
how long
with this masquerade?

There is a chain of fire
stretching
from the sky to the earth -
grasp on to this chain
if your journey is true,
if you seek your true self.

Do not ask
what love is like -
love is a madness!
It submits to the chains -
but not out of ignorance.

Worship love, young man -
love is joy!
Go forward -
you are pure,
you are graceful,
you are true,
I swear.

When your journey
is toward oblivion,
who can obstruct you?
When you are a fire,
raging and pure,
who can withstand you?

Take my spirit
and make it your servant -
breathe life into my life;
Become drunk,
and bring forth!
Once again,
show what it means
to be the creator!

For one moment, one breath
fall silent -
and in that silence, roar.
When you speak,
you are silent -
and in silence
you speak.

To speak
without heart,
without spirit,
is to speak untruths
like the golden calf* -
so travel in truth,
for you are masterful –
you know the way.

*Reference is made to the story of an idol created and worshipped by the Israelites as they wandered in the desert. The story appears in the Bible and the Qor'an.

جان به فدای عاشقان خوش هوسی است عاشقی
عشق پرست ای پسر باد هواست مابقی

از می عشق سرخوشم آتش عشق مفرشم
پای بنه در آتشم چند از این منافقی

از سوی چرخ تا زمین سلسله‌ای است آتشین
سلسله را بگیر اگر در ره خود محققی

عشق مپرس چون بود عشق یکی جنون بود
سلسله را زبون بود نی به طریق احمقی

عشق پرست ای پسر عشق خوش است ای پسر
رو که به جان صادقان صاف و لطیف و صادقی

راه تو چون فنا بود خصم تو را کجا بود
طاقت تو که را بود کاتش تیز مطلقی

جان مرا تو بنده کن عیش مرا تو زنده کن
مست کن و بیافرین بازنمای خالقی

یک نفسی خموش کن در خمشی خروش کن
وقت سخن تو خامشی در خمشی تو ناطقی

بی‌دل و جان سخنوری شیوه گاو سامری
راست نباشد ای پسر برو که حاذقی

{ 21 }

I am a painter,
a sculptor of forms;
every moment,
I create
a new idol -
a beautiful form -
and then,
at your feet,
I set them all ablaze.

I conjure up
a hundred images,
imbue them with spirit,
then
I catch a glimpse of you,
and toss them all
into the fire.

You are the cup-bearer,
the wine-giver,
the scourge of sobriety;
the one who brings to ruin
every house I build.

My life flows
from you, to you;
my essence
is mingled with yours,
and carries your scent -
so I will caress it,
cherish it.

As each new life-form
arises from me,
it speaks onto your core,
and says:
"I bear the color of your kindness;
I share the playground of your love."

{ continued }

صورتگر نقاشم هر لحظه بتی سازم
وانگه همه بتها را در پیش تو بگدازم

صد نقش برانگیزم با روح درآمیزم
چون نقش تو را بینم در آتشش اندازم

تو ساقی خماری یا دشمن هشیاری
یا آنك كنی ویران هر خانه كه می سازم

جان ریخته شد بر تو آمیخته شد با تو
چون بوی تو دارد جان جان را هله بنوازم

هر خون که ز من روید با خاك تو می گوید
با مهر تو همرنگم با عشق تو هنبازم

در خانه ی آب و گل بی‌توست خراب این دل
یا خانه درآ جانا یا خانه بپردازم

{ 21 cont. }

In this house of water and mud,
without you
my heart is in tatters,
yearning...
so enter my house
my love, my life -
or I will fly out
and abandon this house!

{ 22 }

Through you, the soil turns into flesh;
and flesh then comes to think and speak;
through words and thoughts, the hidden realm
becomes pregnant with countless forms.

Each form is borne of an idea,
but it's compressed, frozen within -
when form is traced back to its essence,
its origin will become clear.

Just as, if someone looks at ice
and knows not the essence of ice,
once the ice melts and water flows
he will then surely know its truth.

Think not but beautiful thoughts -
for thoughts are the fiber of forms;
and each form that is beautiful
is woven of beautiful thoughts.

You choose from where to cast your eyes,
and forms of that caliber come;
so forms are borne of your regard;
forms that become women and men.

So sit with those who are with light -
for there is flow from heart to heart!
Grass and lillies grow out of dirt
because the soil dwells with water.

And if you come to dwell with Truth,
you will become pure, joyous life!
How full of splendor you will be -
like the essence of you and me.

From place to no-place, you will come;
distaste will go, wonder will come;
free of arms and legs, you will come -
like the beautiful harvest moon.

{ continued }

ای از تو خاکی تن شده تن فکرت و گفتن شده
وز گفت و فکرت بس صور در غیب آبستن شده

هر صورتی پروردهای معنی است لیک افسردهای
صورت چو معنی شد کنون آغاز را روشن شده

یخ را اگر بیند کسی و آن کس نداند اصل یخ
چون دید کآخر آب شد در اصل یخ بیظن شده

اندیشه جز زیبا مکن کو تار و پود صورت است
ز اندیشهای احسن تند هر صورتی احسن شده

زان سوی کاندازی نظر آن جنس میآید صور
پس از نظر آید صور اشکال مرد و زن شده

با آن نشین کو روشن است کز سوی دل روزن است
خاک از چه ورد و سوسن است کش آب هم مسکن شده

ور همنشین حق شوی جان خوش مطلق شوی
یا رب چه بارونق شوی ای جان جان من شده

از جا به بیجا آمده اه رفته هیهای آمده
بیدست و بیپای آمده چون ماه خوش خرمن شده

یا رب که چون میبینمش ای بنده جان و دینمش
خود چیست این تمکینمش ای عقل از این امکن شده

هر ذرهای را محرم او هر خوش دمی را همدم او
نادیده زو زاهد شده زو دیده تردامن شده

ای عشق حق سودای او آن او است او جویای او
وی میدمد در وای او ای طالب معدن شده

هم طالب و مطلوب او هم عاشق و معشوق او
هم یوسف و یعقوب او هم طوق و هم گردن شده

{ 22 cont. }

When I see her, I'm filled with awe;
my soul's her servant, she's my creed;
all of my praises fall far short;
she makes all knowledge possible.

She's every atom's confidant,
the companion of each joyous breath;
those who haven't beheld her, stray;
and those who have, shed tears of joy.

And those who seek the mine, the source,
the love of Truth their only trade,
she'll be the one to search for them,
and breathe into their songs of love.

She is the seeker and the sought.
She is Lover, and the Beloved.
She is Joseph and Jacob both.
She is the necklace and the neck.

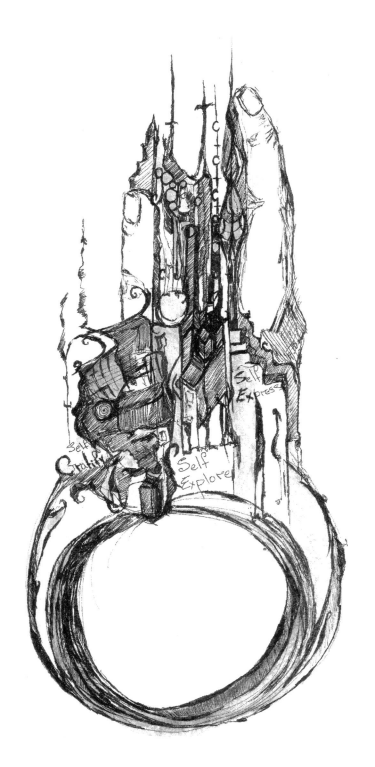

Self
Creation

Self
Explore

Self
Express

{ 23 }

I seek a lover so in love
that every time he rises up,
from every direction he'll raise
insurrections full of fire.

He'll have a heart, inferno-like,
that burns away the flames of hell;
he'll rouse and churn two hundred seas
and will not flee from crashing waves.

He'll wrap the heavens in his hands
and twist them 'round, like so much cloth;
the light of immortality
he'll hang, like an eternal lamp.

He'll come to battle lion-like,
and bring a heart grand as a whale;
he'll battle even with himself,
and leave nothing, except the Self.

And when he shines his light, and tears
the heart's all seven hundred veils,
he'll hear from that celestial throne
the very word of the divine.

When he reaches the seventh sea,
and turns towards the highest peak,
what gems and pearls he'll pour as gifts
from that ocean unto the earth!

مرا عاشق چنان باید که هر باری که برخیزد
قیامتهای پرآتش ز هر سویی برانگیزد

دلی خواهیم چون دوزخ که دوزخ را فروسوزد
دو صد دریا بشوراند ز موج بحر نگریزد

فلکها را چو مندیلی به دست خویش درپیچد
چراغ لایزالی را چو قندیلی درآویزد

چو شیری سوی جنگ آید دل او چون نهنگ آید
بجز خود هیچ نگذارد و با خود نیز بستیزد

چو هفت صد پرده‌ی دل را به نور خود بدراند
ز عرشش این ندا آید بنامیزد بنامیزد

چو او از هفتمین دریا به کوه قاف رو آرد
از آن دریا چه گوهرها کنار خاك درریزد

{ 24 }

Surrounded by curtains of blood,
love cultivates vast gardens;
for lovers, there is so much to be done
in the beautiful realm of unconditional love.

The mind says: "Six directions is the limit,
and there is no beyond."
Love says, "There is - and I've traveled there often."

The mind saw a market
and quickly set up shop;
love has seen, beyond that market,
grand ventures, and boundless opportunities.

So many, guided by truth,
trusting in the essence of love,
have left the pulpits, like Mansur,*
and headed for the gallows.

Those who serve love
clear away grime,
brimming with passion within;
and those who serve the mind
are filled with denial -
their hearts dark and dim.

The mind says,
"Don't step forward, don't lose yourself!
There are only thorns!"
Love says to the mind,
"Those thorns are within you."

Fall silent, and pull the thorn of matter
out from your heart -
so you can see, within yourself,
blooming meadows, and blossoming flowers.

Shams of Tabriz, you are the sun
amidst clouds of words;
when your shining light appears
all speech vanishes.

*Mansur Al-Hallaj was a 9th-C. Persian mystic executed for heresy.

72

در میان پرده‌ی خون عشق را گلزارها
عاشقان را با جمال عشق بی‌چون کارها

عقل گوید شش جهت حدست و بیرون راه نیست
عشق گوید راه هست و رفته‌ام من بارها

عقل بازاری بدید و تاجری آغاز کرد
عشق دیده زان سوی بازار او بازارها

ای بسا منصور پنهان ز اعتماد جان عشق
ترک منبرها بگفته برشده بر دارها

عاشقان دردکش را در درونه ذوق‌ها
عاقلان تیره دل را در درون انکارها

عقل گوید پا منه کاندر فنا جز خار نیست
عشق گوید عقل را کاندر توست آن خارها

هین خمش کن خار هستی را ز پای دل بکن
تا ببینی در درون خویشتن گلزارها

شمس تبریزی تویی خورشید اندر ابر حرف
چون برآمد آفتابت محو شد گفتارها

{ 25 }

Within this world
an opening appeared
into another world -
a world that no mouth
can describe.

Life in that world
is not tainted by fear of death;
its spring
never turns to autumn.

In that world
the doors and walls
speak of myths and legends;
its bricks and stones
recite poetry.

When the owl goes there,
it turns into a peacock.
when the wolf goes there,
it becomes a shepherd.

What does it mean to go there?
A change of state -
not a change of space
from one place to another.

Watch a longtime field of thorns
become a meadow of blooming flowers
by changing its state.

Look at that ancient, static mountain
what a journey it has made
to become a jewel mine.

Wash your hands and face
in the water of ideas -
for the chefs
have laid out
a vast feast.

جهان اندر گشاده شد جهانی
که وصف او نیاید در زبانی

حیاتش را نباشد خوف مرگی
بهارش را نگرداند خزانی

در و دیوار او افسانه گویان
کلوخ و سنگ او اشعار خوانی

چو جغد آنجا رود، طاوس گردد
چو گرگ آنجا رود، گردد شبانی

به رفتن چون بود؟ تبدیل حالی
نه نقلی از مکانی تا مکانی

به خارستان پا بر جای بنگر
ز نقل حال گردد گلستانی

ببین آن صخره پا بر جای مانده
چه سیران کرد، تا شد لعل کانی

بشوی از آب معنی دست و صورت
که طباخان بگستردند خوانی

{ 26 }

When you enter the heart's garden,
you'll emanate the flowers' scent;
when you fly towards the heavens,
your beauty will rival the moon's.

And if it burns you like lamp-oil
you will become the light itself;
you'll be the host of all the feasts,
though yearning will render you thin as a hair.

You'll be
the kingdom and the king;
heaven and heaven's keeper both;
piety and heresy, too;
you'll be the lion and the deer.

From place to no-place you will go,
away from your own body, too -
without your legs, without a horse,
you'll go like water in a stream.

When you are one with heart and spirit,
you'll be evident and hidden both;
you'll take on the nature of wine,
bitter and sweet all at once.

Freed from the realm of wet and dry,
you'll fly above it all like Christ;
you'll tear up all the maelstroms
and give direction to the waters' flow.

You'll sweeten all that tastes of salt;
you'll make present the far-away;
you won't be a veil unto the light
if you become ninefold,
like the sky.

Be sovereign: make your own wealth;
be as the moon, raise yourself high -
how long, like a cuckoo bird
will you keep searching here and there?

(continued)

چون درشوی در باغ دل ماند گل خوش بو شوی
چون برپری سوی فلك همچون ملك مه رو شوی

گر همچو روغن سوزدت خود روشنی كردی همه
سرخیل عشرت‌ها شوی گر چه ز غم چون مو شوی

هم ملك و هم سلطان شوی هم خلد و هم رضوان شوی
هم كفر و هم ایمان شوی هم شیر و هم آهو شوی

از جای در بی‌جا روی وز خویشتن تنها روی
بی‌مرکب و بی‌پا روی چون آب اندر جو شوی

چون جان و دل یكتا شوی پیدای ناپیدا شوی
هم تلخ و هم حلوا شوی با طبع می همخو شوی

از طبع خشكی و تری همچون مسیحا برپری
گرداب‌ها را بردری راهی كنی یك سو شوی

شیرین كنی هر شور را حاضر كنی هر دور را
پرده نباشی نور را گر چون فلك نه تو شوی

شه باش دولت ساخته مه باش رفعت یافته
تا چند همچون فاخته جوینده و كوكو شوی

خالی كنی سر از هوس گردی تو زنده بی‌نفس
یاهو نگویی زان سپس چون غرقه یاهو شوی

هر خانه را روزن شوی هر باغ را گلشن شوی
با من نباشی من شوی چون تو ز خود بی‌تو شوی

دیگر نخواهی روشنی از خویشتن گردی غنی
چون شاه مسكین پروری چون ماه ظلمت جو شوی

تو جان نخواهی جان دهی هر درد را درمان دهی
مرهم نجویی زخم را خود زخم را دارو شوی

Your head devoid of whims and wants;
you'll be alive without a breath;
no longer calling out to god
when you're immersed in the divine.

You'll be a window to each house,
and every garden's flower-bed;
you won't be with me -
you'll *be* me,
if you come apart from yourself.

Filled to the brim with your own wealth,
you'll no longer search for light -
but like the moon,
you'll seek darkness
and like the King,
you'll seek the poor.

You won't cling to life -
you'll give life;
you will bring healing to all pain;
instead of tending your own wound,
you'll give yourself,
to heal all wounds.

{ 27 }

Die, die
into this love, die;
once you die into this love
you can receive
the spirit
in full.

Die, die,
and don't fear this death -
for you shall rise from this soil
dancing in joy!

Die, die
and detach from this self -
for this self is a chain
and you are like prisoners.

Take hold of an axe
and pierce your way out -
when you break free of this prison
you are rulers, you are kings.

Die, die
before that beautiful king -
once you die before him
you are sovereign,
worthy of legend.

Die, die
and come out from behind this cloud -
once you abandon this cloud
you are the brilliant moon, in full
lighting the way.

Silence, silence,
for silence is the breath of this death -
when you roar in silence
what speaks
is Life itself.

بمیرید بمیرید در این عشق بمیرید
در این عشق چو مردید همه روح پذیرید

بمیرید بمیرید و زین مرگ مترسید
کز این خاک برآیید سماوات بگیرید

بمیرید بمیرید و زین نفس ببرید
که این نفس چو بندست و شما همچو اسیرید

یکی تیشه بگیرید پی حفره‌ی زندان
چو زندان بشکستید همه شاه و امیرید

بمیرید بمیرید به پیش شه زیبا
بر شاه چو مردید همه شاه و شهیرید

بمیرید بمیرید و زین ابر برآیید
چو زین ابر برآیید همه بدر منیرید

خموشید خموشید خموشی دم مرگست
هم از زندگیست اینک ز خاموش نفیرید

{ 28 }

How blissful, that moment:
you and I sitting on the veranda
in two forms,
but of one essence
you and I.

The flowing water of life
brings order to the garden
and gives voice to the birds
when we enter the meadow
you and I.

The planets and stars
come to gaze upon us
and we will show them
our own moon
you and I.

You and I
free from you and I
join together in passion -
joyful,
free of distressing thoughts
and false beliefs
you and I.

The heavenly parrots
will find sugar in their beaks
when we laugh in that way
you and I.

And even more woundrous:
you and I
in this corner, intimately -
and at the same moment
in the West, and in the East,
you and I.

In one form, on this earth -
and in another,
in sweet, eternal paradise
you and I.

{ ۲۸ }

خنک آن دم که نشینیم در ایوان من و تو
به دو نقش و به دو صورت به یکی جان من و تو

داد باغ و دم مرغان بدهد آب حیات
آن زمانی که درآییم به بستان من و تو

اختران فلک آیند به نظاره ما
مه خود را بنماییم بدیشان من و تو

من و تو بی من و تو جمع شویم از سر ذوق
خوش و فارغ ز خرافات پریشان من و تو

طوطیان فلکی جمله شکرخوار شوند
در مقامی که بخندیم بدان سان من و تو

این عجبتر که من و تو به یکی کنج این جا
هم در این دم به عراقیم و خراسان من و تو

به یکی نقش بر این خاک و بر آن نقش دگر
در بهشت ابدی و شکرستان من و تو

{ 29 }

You are
the precious light
in the eyes of mind and soul;
you rule
upon the heart's throne;
like a hundred thousand moons
and a hundred thousand suns
you shine
without a sky.

Stillness and movement are you;
oneness and many are you;
below and above are you;
body and soul are you.

Mountain and desert are you;
pearl and ocean, you;
like spring in the garden,
in the leaves
and in the meadows,
you.

You are
the life within our bodies,
and the life within all lives;
you are
surface and meaning,
the sign and the signified -
apparent, and invisible.

You are
the very being of the world,
and the existence of humans;
hundreds of earths and skies,
an infinite labyrinth.

You are one,
but turned your Self into infinite shapes -
how can I not see you,
when you are here
in thousands of forms?

Day and night I sought you,
speaking your name,
praising you;
and when I opened my eyes,
I saw
that even the seeker
is you.

Those who haven't seen you
cannot speak of this -
they burst with terror
at the very thought...
but it's you
who says these words,
not me -
for within me,
what speaks
is you.

ای نور چشم عقل و جان بر تخت دل سلطان تویی
چون صد هزاران ماه و خور بی آسمان تابان تویی

هم ساکن و جنبان تویی یکسان تویی صد سان تویی
پستی تویی بالا تویی هم تن تویی هم جان تویی

هم کوه و هم صحرا تویی هم گوهر و دریا تویی
همچون بهار اندر چمن دربرگ و دربستان تویی

در جسم ما چون جان تویی در جان‌ها جانان تویی
صورت تویی معنی تویی پیدا تویی پنهان تویی

هم هستی عالم تویی هم هستی آدم تویی
صد چون زمین و آسمان در ظل بی پایان تویی

خود را نمودی ای احد اندر نقوش بی عدد
چون که نمی‌بینم تو را اندر هزاران سان تویی

جویان بدم روز و شبت در ذکر گویان یا ربت
چون باز کردم دیده را دیدم که هم جویان تویی

نادیده کس کی گوید این زهره ش درد از خوف این
این را تو میگویی نه من چون در زبان گویان تویی

{ 30 }

Look, herdsman:
see the drunken camels -
an endless procession
in both directions!
The king is drunk,
the princes are drunk,
friends are drunk,
and strangers too.

Look, gardener:
thunder becomes the musician,
clouds bring the wine -
and so,
the garden is drunk,
the meadow is drunk,
blossoms are drunk,
and thorns are too.

Look, sky -
how long do you turn!
Watch the turning of the elements:
water is drunk,
wind is drunk,
soil is drunk,
and fire too.

If the realm of form
is in such a state,
then how is the realm of ideas?
Don't ask!
Spirit is drunk,
consciousness is drunk,
mysteries are drunk,
and perception too.

Don't say that in winter
the garden is left sober -
the drunks are only hiding
for a while,
away from treacherous eyes.

(continued)

ساربانا اشتران بین سر به سر قطار مست
میر مست و خواجه مست و یار مست اغیار مست

باغبانا رعد مطرب ابر ساقی گشت و شد
باغ مست و راغ مست و غنچه مست و خار مست

آسمانا چند گردی گردش عنصر ببین
آب مست و باد مست و خاك مست و نار مست

حال صورت این چنین و حال معنی خود مپرس
روح مست و عقل مست و وهم مست اسرار مست

تا نگویی در زمستان باغ را مستی نماند
مدتی پنهان شدست از دیده مکار مست

بیخهای آن درختان می نهانی میخورند
روزکی دو صبر میکن تا شود بیدار مست

گر تو را کوبی رسد از رفتن مستان مرنج
با چنان ساقی و مطرب کی رود هموار مست

شمس تبریزی به دورت هیچ کس هشیار نیست
کافر و مومن خراب و زاهد و خمار مست

{ 30 cont. }

But the roots of those trees
are secretly drinking wine ...
just wait, a day or two,
and the drunks will awaken.

So if you suffer a blow or two
from this drunken procession,
don't take offense...
with such a wine-giver
and such musicians,
how could the drunkards
march in a straight line?

Shams of Tabriz,
in your presence
no one is left sober...
the pious are drunk,
and heretics, too;
ascetics are drunk
and wine-sellers too.

{ 31 }

Of whom should I be afraid
when the Beloved is with me?
Why be scared of the needles
when that great sword is with me?

Why would my mouth remain dry
when that great river seeks me?
My companion swallows grief -
so why would my heart feel sad?

Why would I taste bitterness,
immersed in sugar and sweets?
How could winter penetrate
when that new Spring is with me?

Why burn and cry with fever
when Christ is here to heal me?
Why be afraid of the dogs
when the hunt-master's with me?

Why would I not join the feast -
the wine-giver draws me in!
Why would I not conquer states
when that great ruler's with me?

In that noble royal cask,
crimson wine ferments for us -
so how could I suffer here,
thirsty and yearning for wine?

If I defy the great wheel,
break it down, toss it about,
why should I need to explain -
when that beauty is with me?

In blessings I am immersed,
joyful in kindness and grace;
with that lovely companion,
fortune's always at my side.

You
who roars these drunken words:
I'm done with speeches and talk;
quiet down,
and hold your tongue -
or else do not speak with me.

من از کی باك دارم خاصه که یار با من
از سوزنی چه ترسم و آن ذوالفقار با من

کی خشك لب بمانم كان جو مراست جویان
كی غم خورد دل من وآن غمگسار با من

تلخی چرا کشم من من غرق قند و حلوا
در من کجا رسد دی و آن نوبهار با من

از تب چرا خروشم عیسی طبیب هوشم
وز سگ چرا هراسم میر شکار با من

در بزم چون نیایم ساقیم می‌کشاند
چون شهرها نگیرم وآن شهریار با من

در خم خسروانی می بهر ماست جوشان
این جا چه کار دارد رنج خمار با من

با چرخ اگر ستیزم ور بشکنم بریزم
عذرم چه حاجت آید وآن خوش عذار با من

من غرق ملك و نعمت سرمست لطف و رحمت
اندر کنار بختم وآن خوش کنار با من

ای ناطقه معربد از گفت سیر گشتم
خاموش کن وگر نی صحبت مدار با من

{ 32 }

There is someone hidden here,
tugging at my skirt;
she holds herself back,
and guides me forward.

There is someone hidden here,
delicate as spirit,
and even lovelier;
she's revealed to me a garden,
and sits, regally, on my veranda.

There is someone hidden here,
like a vision in the heart;
yet the radiant light of her face
has penetrated my roots.

There is someone hidden here,
like sugar in the cane;
a sweet merchant of sweets
has taken over my shop.

A magician, a conjurer,
unseen by the eyes;
a skilful trader
has taken over my scales.

She and I are mingled together
like sugar and flowers;
I've taken her scent
and she's taken my all.

All the virtues of this world
are as nothing in my eyes -
for visions of her
cling to my eyelashes.

Bruised and battered,
I circled the world
and found no cure -
until love's yearning
came to heal me.

Your heart is aching too, I see,
and you'll be cured of that ache
if you can grasp what I say.

In the sea of despair,
if you sever yourself from greed,
you'll emerge from the water
with precious coral in your hands.

Shatter the spell of forms;
open your sated eyes,
and you will see,
East and West
ruled by my King.

You'll see clearly
the invisible cup-bearer,
the object of my devotion,
holding the grand goblet
and beckoning you...

{ Note: This is a segment of a longer poem. }

این جا کسی است پنهان دامان من گرفته
خود را سپس کشیده پیشان من گرفته

این جا کسی است پنهان چون جان و خوشتر از جان
باغی به من نموده ایوان من گرفته

این جا کسی است پنهان همچون خیال در دل
اما فروغ رویش ارکان من گرفته

این جا کسی است پنهان مانند قند در نی
شیرین شکرفروشی دکان من گرفته

جادو و چشم بندی چشم کسش نبیند
سوداگری است موزون میزان من گرفته

چون گلشکر من و او در همدگر سرشته
من خوی او گرفته او آن من گرفته

در چشم من نیاید خوبان جمله عالم
بنگر خیال خوبش مژگان من گرفته

من خسته گرد عالم درمان ز کس ندیدم
تا درد عشق دیدم درمان من گرفته

تو نیز دل کبابی درمان ز درد یابی
گر گرد درد گردی فرمان من گرفته

در بحر ناامیدی از خود طمع بریدی
زین بحر سر برآری مرجان من گرفته

بشکن طلسم صورت بگشای چشم سیرت
تا شرق و غرب بینی سلطان من گرفته

ساقی غیب بینی پیدا سلام کرده
پیمانه جام کرده پیمان من گرفته

{ 33 }

You, who pass through this mortal world
riding upon the horse of immortality:
you are wise,
you see the way,
you follow your knowingness.

Not burdened by physicality,
not lured by any baits and traps --
freeing yourself from disappointment,
you travel
into fulfillment.

Not like reason, petty and small,
not like ego, full of spite,
not like the earthly animal spirit --
you travel
as pure life-force.

Woven of heavenly thread,
brilliant like the moon;
you've found the path
and journey
into the unseen.

Immersed in thoughts of the Beloved,
having lost your self in her wine,
you travel
from her School of Names
into the realm of ideas.

Your temperament,
like spring water,
has added its scent, its color, to the earth -
so that no one will think
that you leave
without leaving your mark.

Each night, caravans travel up,
rising from this world towards the sky;
but you, singular Self,
you travel
as a hundred caravans.

(continued)

ای آن که بر اسب بقا از دیر فانی می‌روی
دانا و بینای رهی آن سو که دانی می‌روی

بی‌همره جسم و عرض بی‌دام و دانه و بی‌غرض
از تلخکامی می‌رهی در کامرانی می‌روی

نی همچو عقل دانه چین نی همچو نفس پر ز کین
نی روح حیوان زمین تو جان جانی می‌روی

ای چون فلک دربافته ای همچو مه درتافته
از ره نشانی یافته در بی‌نشانی می‌روی

ای غرقه‌ی سودای او ای بیخود از صهبای او
از مدرسه اسمای او اندر معانی می‌روی

ای خوی تو چون آب جو داده زمین را رنگ و بو
تا کس نپندارد که تو بی‌ارمغانی می‌روی

کو سایه‌ی منصور حق تا فاش فرماید سبق
کز مستعینی می‌رهی در مستعانی می‌روی

شب کاروان‌ها زین جهان بر می‌رود تا آسمان
تو خود به تنهایی خود صد کاروانی می‌روی

ای آفتاب آن جهان در ذره‌ای چونی نهان
وی پادشاه شه نشان در پاسبانی می‌روی

ای بس طلسمات عجب بستی برون از روز و شب
تا چشم پندارد که تو اندر مکانی می‌روی

ای لطف غیبی چند تو شکل بهاری می‌شوی
وی عدل مطلق چند تو اندر خزانی می‌روی

آخر برون آ زین صور چادر برون افکن ز سر
تا چند در رنگ بشر در گله بانی می‌روی

ای ظاهر و پنهان چو جان وی چاکر و سلطان چو جان
کی بینمت پنهان چو جان در بی‌زبانی می‌روی

{ 33 cont. }

O otherworldly sun:
how do you hide
inside a particle?
O great King and kingmaker:
how do you travel
as a guardsman?

So many wondrous spells you've cast
outside the realm of day and night,
so that the eyes will think
that you travel
within space.

O invisible grace,
how long
will you take the form of Spring?
O pure justice,
how long
will you take the guise of Autumn?

Come out,
come out from behind the forms;
let the veil fall off your head!
How long
in human color
will you travel,
guiding the flock?

Visible and invisible, as spirit;
servant and king, as spirit;
when will I see you,
o hidden spirit,
traveling silently
beyond words...?

{ 34 }

I went on a journey
without me;
and there,
my heart bloomed
without me.

That beauty
who always evaded me
touched her face to mine
without me.

In yearning for her
I gave up my life,
and in that yearning
I was reborn
without me.

Now,
I am perpetually drunk
without wine;
forever in joy
without me.

Erase me from memory -
for I remember myself
without me.

Without myself
I've found joy;
and so I declare:
may I remain, eternally
without me.

All the doors
were closed unto me;
but they opened
once she invited me in
without me.

I am set free
from good and from bad;
liberated
from oppression
and from corruption -
without me.

I am drunk
from the cup of Shams;
may his goblet of wine
never be
without me.

ما را سفری فتاد بی ما
آنجا دل ما گشاد بی ما

آن مه که ز ما نهان همی شد
رُخ بر رُخ ما نهاد بی ما

چون در غم دوست جان بدادیم
ما را غم او بزاد بی ما

ماییم همیشه مست بی می
ماییم همیشه شاد بی ما

ما را مکنید یاد هرگز
ما خود هستیم یاد بی ما

بی ما شده ایم شاد گوئیم
ای ما که همیشه باد بی ما

در ها همه بسته بود بر ما
بگشود چو راه داد بی ما

ماییم ز نیک و بد رهیده
از طاعت و از فساد بی ما

مستیم ز جام شمس تبریز
جام می او مباد بی ما

Published by YOUniversal Center
Los Angeles, California

69948555R00058

Made in the USA
San Bernardino, CA
22 February 2018